T*A*P*S

is

Survivors Helping Survivors Heal

A Kid's Journey of Grief
official T*A*P*S edition

A coloring and activity book for children of military families
who never chose to travel down the path of grief,
but, nevertheless, find themselves on this road.

Many thanks to our wonderful supporters who truly care about
our military family and have contributed to this book's success:

CACI
CIBC World Markets
TriWest Healthcare Alliance

Contact us for more information:

T.A.P.S.
1777 F Street, N.W., Suite 600
Washington D.C. 20006
800-959-TAPS (8277)
Website: www.taps.org
Email: info@taps.org

Vision Unlimited Publishers
3832 Radnor Avenue, Long Beach, CA 90808
Phone: 562-421-1717
Email: info@akidsjourneyofgrief.org

ISBN # 0-9746385-2-8

A Message from our Friends at
TriWest Healthcare Alliance

At TriWest Healthcare Alliance, military families aren't just our customers. They're our inspiration. Our motivation. Our heroes. Every day, we are humbled by the strength, commitment and patriotism of our nation's military families—for we know that they too dedicate themselves in service to this country. We also know that with their service comes great sacrifice and, regrettably in some instances, great loss.

As the Department of Defense contractor responsible for managing the TRICARE program in the 21-state West Region, we are committed to meeting the physical and emotional health care needs of these brave families not only through our work, but also through our corporate support of programs and services designed uniquely for them. It is for this reason that we are most honored to sponsor the efforts of the Tragedy Assistance Program for Survivors (TAPS)—and, in turn, this workbook, which leads children grieving the loss of a loved one on a thoughtful, healing journey.

It is our sincere hope that, through the strength of this book and the unparalleled support of TAPS, grieving military families might find comfort and peace during their time of sorrow. As an organization, and as members of the American community, we are infinitely grateful for the sacrifices of the men and women who wear our nation's uniform and their families. Our hearts, our prayers and our work are focused squarely on them.

David J. McIntyre, Jr.
TriWest Healthcare Alliance
President and CEO

From Our Hearts to Yours
May 2005

Any child who has learned to love will experience grief when someone special in his or her life dies. For years, it has been our passion to give children an opportunity to grieve effectively after the death of a loved one. Since 1994, TAPS has conducted the *Good Grief Camp for Young Survivors*, and offered the children of those who have died while serving in the military the chance to come together to learn ways to cope with their grief, make friends who truly understood their pain, and participate in Memorial Day ceremonies to understand the wonderful ways America honors all those who make the ultimate sacrifice for freedom.

We are so glad that you have this copy of our handbook for grieving children. It was created with love after many years of careful research, complete with coloring pages, activities, and a little frog to help children on their way. It is used during the TAPS Good Grief Camp, and is also a wonderful resource for children to use with the supervision of an adult.

The material is based on the model of grief developed by Dr. J. William Worden. In his books, *Children and Grief and Grief Counseling* and *Grief Therapy*, Dr. Worden identified "four tasks" that everyone who mourns must accomplish: (1) accept the reality of the death of your special person, (2) experience the pain of your grief, (3) adjust to an environment in which the deceased is no longer present, and (4) emotionally relocate the deceased in your heart and move on with life to a "new normal." His model was adopted as the foundation for the teachings in this children's book.

The purpose and desire for this handbook is that each child who uses it would be able to move forward successfully on his or her own journey through grief. So, it is from our hearts to yours that we provide this "map" for the personal journey of the grieving child in your life. May it bring healing and new hope.

Susan K. Beeney, R.N. (Co-Author)

Jo Anne Chung, B.S.R.N. (Co-Author and Illustrator)

Lieutenant Colonel Judith Mathewson, USAF
M.S., M.Ed., Grief Counselor, TAPS Good Grief Camp Director

Jena Moore, M.F.T., TAPS Youth Programs

How To Use This Book Effectively

Who should use this book?
- ☆ Children who have suffered the death of a military person in their lives
- ☆ It is not intended to be used in any circumstances of loss or change other than the loss of life.

For what age group is this book appropriate?
- ☆ Boys and girls between the ages of 5 and 12 years old

Can a child go through this book on his/her own?
- ☆ The younger child needs an adult to help with reading and understanding the material.
- ☆ The older child can use this book with minimal adult assistance.
- ☆ This book is intended to be used as a springboard for discussion with a child. Talking about feelings is an important part of a child's grieving process.

How long should it take for a grieving child to go through this book?
- ☆ Each child needs to work through personal grief at his/her own pace.
- ☆ This book is not meant to be completed in one or two sittings, but over a period of time to allow the child to understand and verbalize feelings about his/her grief.

Can this book be used in a group setting?
- ☆ Yes. It can be used by either a single child (assisted by an adult) or a group of children (led by an adult).
- ☆ It is used at the T☆A☆P☆S **GOOD GRIEF CAMP FOR YOUNG SURVIVORS.**

In what kind of settings can I use this book?
- ☆ In the home, with a parent, guardian or relative.
- ☆ In professional counseling with clients.
- ☆ In small grief groups for children:
  - ➤ through family support groups
  - ➤ through a school counselor
  - ➤ through hospitals or hospice
  - ➤ through a church or with a chaplain
- ☆ In any setting where the death of a military member has affected a common community of children (i.e. the death of a teacher, classmate, or principal at an elementary school).
- ☆ In summary, this book is valuable in <u>any</u> individual or group situations in which children need to share and work through their grief.

How adults can help children deal with death and grief
12 IMPORTANT INTERVENTIONS
FOR THE GRIEVING CHILD

1. Bereaved kids need to know that they will be cared for, and that their family is still a family, even without the deceased person.

2. Bereaved kids often have feelings of guilt and need to know that they did not cause the death.

3. Bereaved kids need very clear information about the death, the causes, and the circumstances. Give information in age-appropriate words.

4. Normal routines of activity and home life need to be maintained or reestablished.

5. Kids need someone who will answer questions. Often they need a surrogate person if a parent has died.

6. Reminiscing about the deceased person with others is helpful. Share the difficult memories as well as the fun and loving ones. Encourage kids to ask questions. Respond with simple, concise answers.

7. Grieving reactions are often spontaneous. Allow them to express their grief through their play, art, and behavior. Remain consistent in your discipline to maintain the safe boundaries that kids need.

8. Model your grief for them by not hiding your emotions or your ways of expressing your grief.

9. Tell the child to expect some or all of these feelings as they grieve: anger, sadness, fear, guilt. Children need to be assured that these are normal, expected emotions of grief. Allow the child to freely and safely express these feelings.

10. Each child will have feelings and behaviors that express his or her grief individually. Some will cry a lot. Others will not. Some will talk about the death. Others will grieve privately. Some grieve for months and months. Others may return to "normal" fairly quickly. Make sure that the children know it is OK to feel whatever they are feeling and that they will be accepted where they are in the grief process.

11. Children need to be able to express feelings of anger in safe non-harmful ways. Some suggestions are:
    - throwing ice cubes at a fence
    - tossing *Nerf* balls at an object
    - ripping tissue out of the box
    - punching a pillow or screaming into a pillow
    - tearing pages out of a magazine or telephone book
    - popping bubble wrap

12. A child's grief begins when he/she begins to express or demonstrate his/her feelings.

This book is about my grief journey when my special person died.

Draw a picture of your special person.

My special person was _____.(name)

She/he was my _____. (Relationship to you)

She/he died on _____. (month, day, year)

My name is _____. This is me, in
my normal life before _____ died.
(your special person)

Then my _____ died and life turned upside down!

I feel so _____!!

It doesn't feel like life will ever be normal again.

Draw a face to show how you feel.

Tell someone about the feelings you had on the day of the funeral, or memorial service or at the graveside.

THERE ARE NO WRONG FEELINGS WHEN YOU ARE GRIEVING.

(Use lots of your favorite colors to color this page.)

The feelings that you feel when someone you care about dies are called

GRIEF

When someone you love dies, your journey begins and grief is the path you must travel.

GRIEF

My journey of grief began when _____ died.

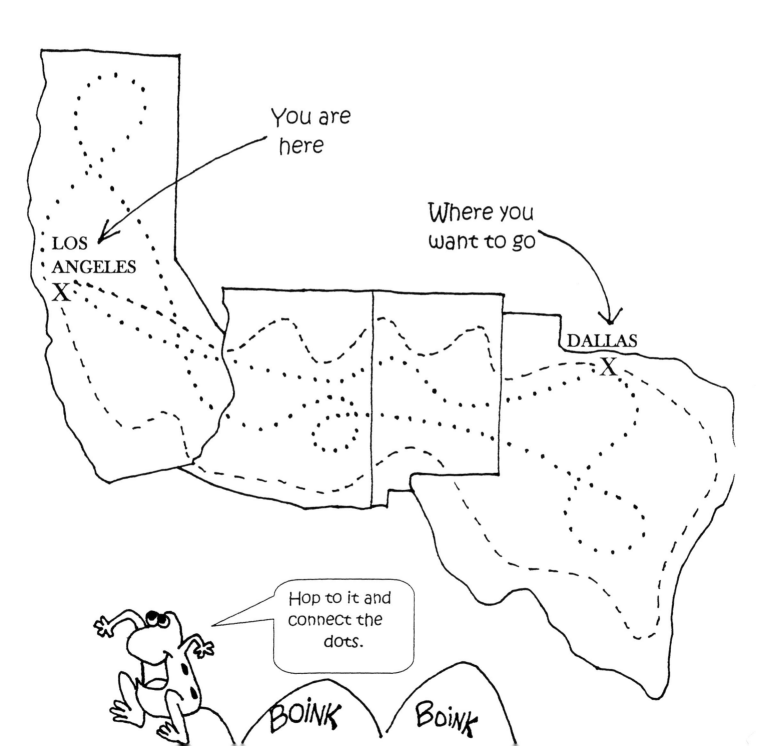

YOU NEED A MAP!

A map will show you where you <u>are</u> and where you <u>need to go</u>.

But, you are on a journey of grief

THE LANDS

It shows you where you are, and where

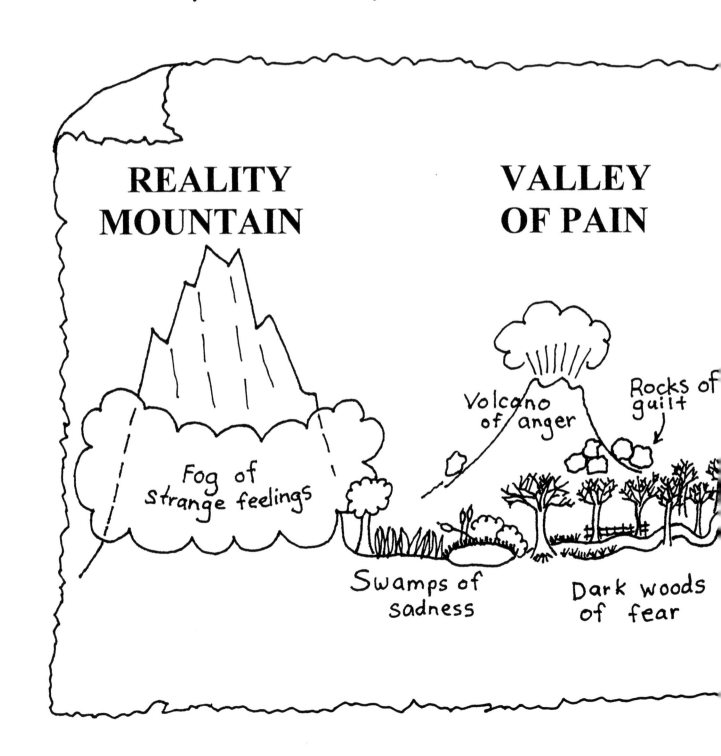

REALITY MOUNTAIN

VALLEY OF PAIN

Fog of Strange feelings

Volcano of anger

Rocks of guilt

Swamps of sadness

Dark woods of fear

and you need the map of

OF MOURNING

you need to go during this sad time.

HILLS OF CHANGE

SPRINGS OF NEW NORMAL

Big Changes

Little Changes

Feeling happy again
Enjoying friends
Having fun

Long desert of grief

This is the first land
through which you need to travel.

REALITY MOUNTAIN

You need to pass through the . . .

VALLEY OF PAIN

And you need to travel
up and down the . . .
HILLS OF CHANGE

But, sooner or later,
you will get to the. . .

SPRINGS OF
NEW NORMAL

Everyone who is on the grief journey must travel through these lands to get through their grief.

THERE ARE <u>NO DETOURS</u>!

But there are many different paths you can choose to get from one land to another.

The path <u>you</u> take will depend on the <u>feelings</u> you have.

On your grief journey, you will have many strong feelings because of the death of your special person. All your feelings are <u>normal</u> and need to be felt.

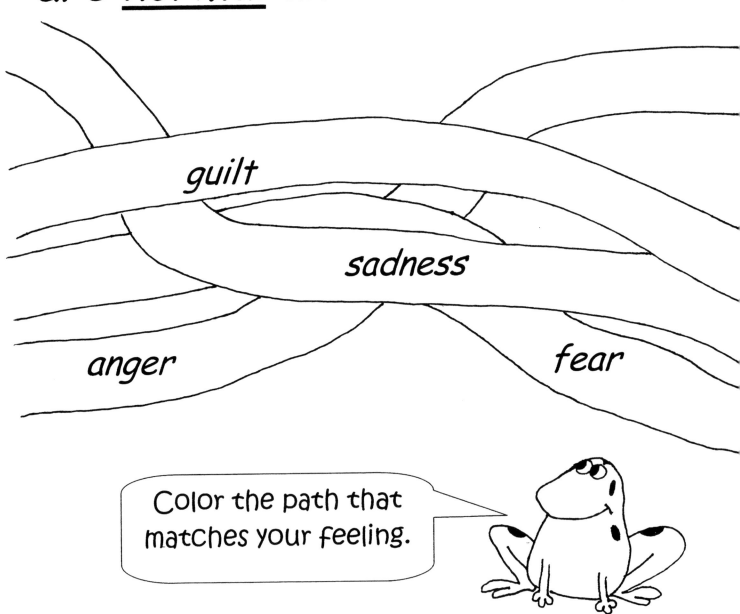

guilt

sadness

anger

fear

Color the path that matches your feeling.

YOU START YOUR GRIEF JOURNEY ON

This is where you must begin to face the truth that your special person has died and is not coming back.

It's hard to face the truth that _____ has died.

(put your special person's name here)

It may feel like you are in a

FOG OF STRANGE FEELINGS.

I can't find my lilly pad!

In the beginning when that special person has died, many kids feel . . .

SHOCK,

"But he wasn't supposed to die!"

"It was an accident. I did not expect that!"

"Oh no!"

"What terrible news!"

DISBELIEF,

CONFUSION

LACK OF
CONCENTRATION,

RELIEF,

And some kids even FEEL or ACT LIKE a BABY.

But these FEELINGS and WAYS OF ACTING are **<u>NORMAL</u>**, and they won't last.

It's just because you are a grieving kid.

But even when you are grieving, you can have a

GOOD DAY

_____ would want me to feel these good feelings.

where you have fun and feel happy. <u>This is normal, too</u>. Enjoy these good days full of laughter and happiness.

Match the feelings that you may feel when you are going through the FOG OF STRANGE FEELINGS.

Disbelief

Happy

Lack of Concentration
    or Confusion

Nothing at All

Relief

    Feeling or
Acting Like a Baby

Shock

(Color in the faces that <u>you</u> are feeling)

ANOTHER LAND OF MOURNING IS THE VALLEY OF PAIN.
IN THIS LAND, YOU MAY FEEL MANY STRONG FEELINGS AND CRY A LOT.

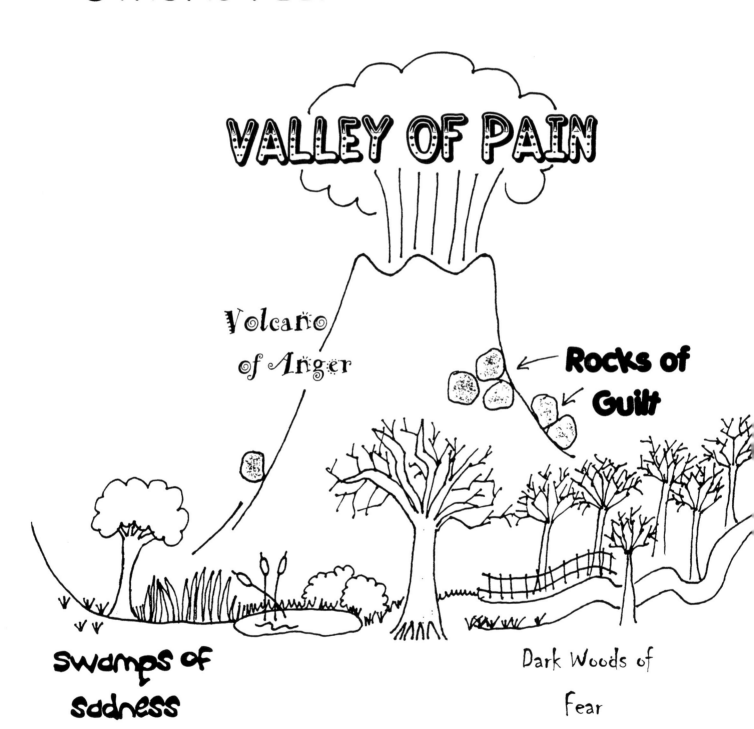

You may feel <u>sad</u>, <u>angry</u>, <u>guilty</u>, <u>afraid</u> or even <u>happy</u> . . . or you may have other feelings.

angry

guilty

sad

afraid

happy

_____

my feeling now

Draw your face to show how you are feeling.

On your grief journey, you may find yourself feeling very sad. When you are feeling this way, you have stopped in the **swamps of sadness.**

When you feel sad,
it is good to cry
(even if nobody else is crying).

Three of these children are showing sadness.
Three of these children are not. Circle the three
children who are showing what it's like to be sad
because someone died.

Color the children who are showing the way
you feel sadness.

Tell someone else what your sadness feels like. You could tell . . .

A Parent

A Friend

A Teacher

Draw the person that you will tell.

or, maybe

get a hug

from someone
who cares about you.

While in the valley of pain, you may feel angry. When you feel this way, you have climbed the

VOLCANO
OF ANGER
Yikes!

And you may not know when it's going to blow!

(Color the lava red and the smoke gray)

Have you ever felt so angry that you wanted to punch somebody?

Punching polliwogs! Circle and color the picture of the child who is showing her anger in a way that doesn't harm herself or anyone else.

When your special person died,
you could not prevent his (or her) death.
You might feel helpless or powerless.
This may lead you to feel angry.

Draw how you look when you feel angry.

It is _normal_ to feel this way.

Sometimes kids hide their feelings when they are grieving.

COLOR THE BLOCKS TO REVEAL A HIDDEN PICTURE. 1=red 2=brown   3=blue   4=tan

It is important to tell others your feelings.

Holding in your angry feelings is like trying to put a cork in a

volcaño

to stop it from exploding!

There are many ways to get your angry feelings out. You could . . .

☑ Check the ones you like best. Personally, I like throwing socks!

☐ --------------------------------- Tear out tissues from a box.

☐ --------------------------------- Punch and scream into pillows.

☐ --------------------------------- Tear up old magazines.

☐ --------------------------------- Run in a game like tag or soccer.

☐ --------------------------------- Practice jumping rope.

☐ --------------------------------- Throw sock balls into the closet.

☐ --------------------------------- Have a family paper ball fight.

☐ ---------------------------------

(Come up with your own idea)

It feels <u>SO</u> <u>GOOD</u> to get the anger* out.

*But, remember . . .
when you get the anger
out, don't hurt yourself
and don't hurt others.

Draw a picture of you getting your anger out.

WHILE IN THE VALLEY OF PAIN, YOU MAY GET LOST IN THE

DARK WOODS of FEAR

I'm glad teddy is with us!

Since the death
of your special person,
you may feel new fears
along this path of
grief, such as. . .

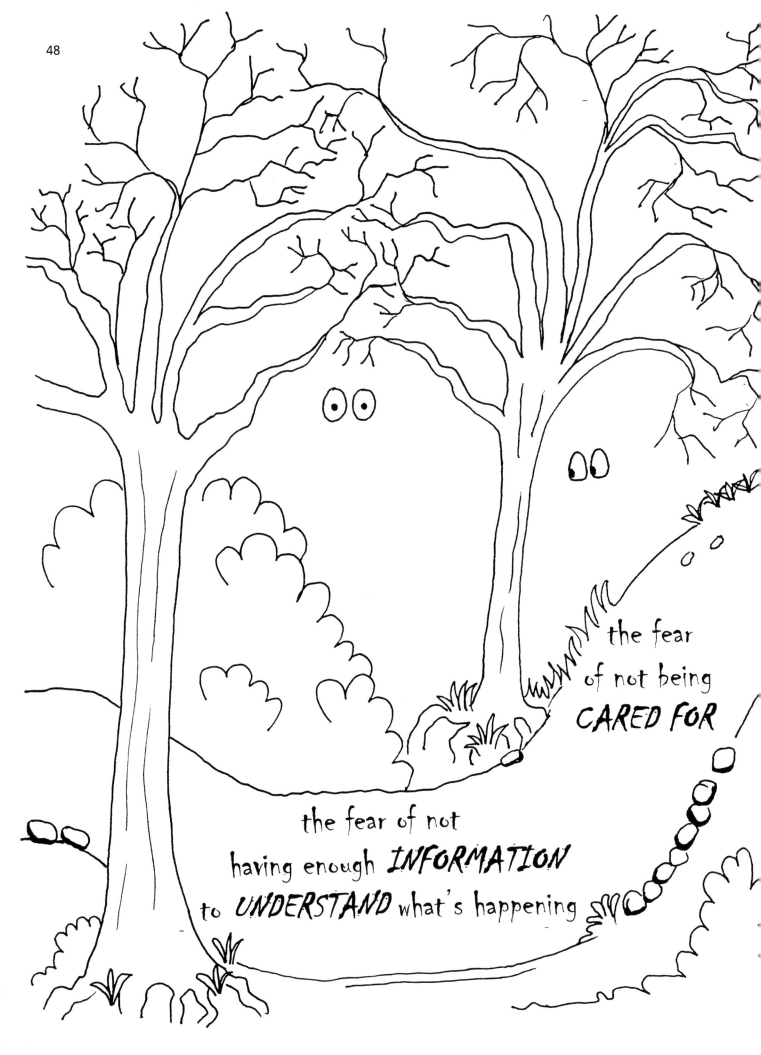

the fear of not being **CARED FOR**

the fear of not having enough **INFORMATION** to **UNDERSTAND** what's happening

the fear that
you are to *BLAME*

the *FEAR* that
another special
person may *DIE*

the fear that you may *NEVER*
be as *SPECIAL* to someone else
as you were to the one who died

WORD SEARCH

Circle the following words from the path of the Dark Woods of Fear:

INFORMATION, UNDERSTAND, CARED FOR, BLAME, FEAR, DIE, NEVER, SPECIAL

Search up, down, across and diagonally.

(Having trouble finding the words? Go to the back of this book for the answers.)

U	P	O	C	S	I	D	Z	F	U	S	A
A	N	Y	A	O	V	C	Q	E	G	P	K
W	E	D	R	I	R	B	L	A	M	E	M
C	V	A	E	K	M	H	D	R	M	C	W
V	E	P	D	R	D	C	K	R	D	I	E
U	R	F		N	S	W	X	F	R	A	M
M	J	Z		U	E	T	Z	T	Q	L	K
K	I	N	F	O	R	M	A	T	I	O	N
D	F	T	O	S	K	C	M	N	F	R	T
X	C	N	R	L	X	A	G	E	D	J	K

What are you afraid of?

Write down your fears
since your special person died.

I am scared that _____

_____

_____

_____

_____

_____

_____

_____

Tell someone you trust about your fears.
He or she may be able to help you
deal with them.

Know that there are many people around you that care about you. Some of them may be. . .

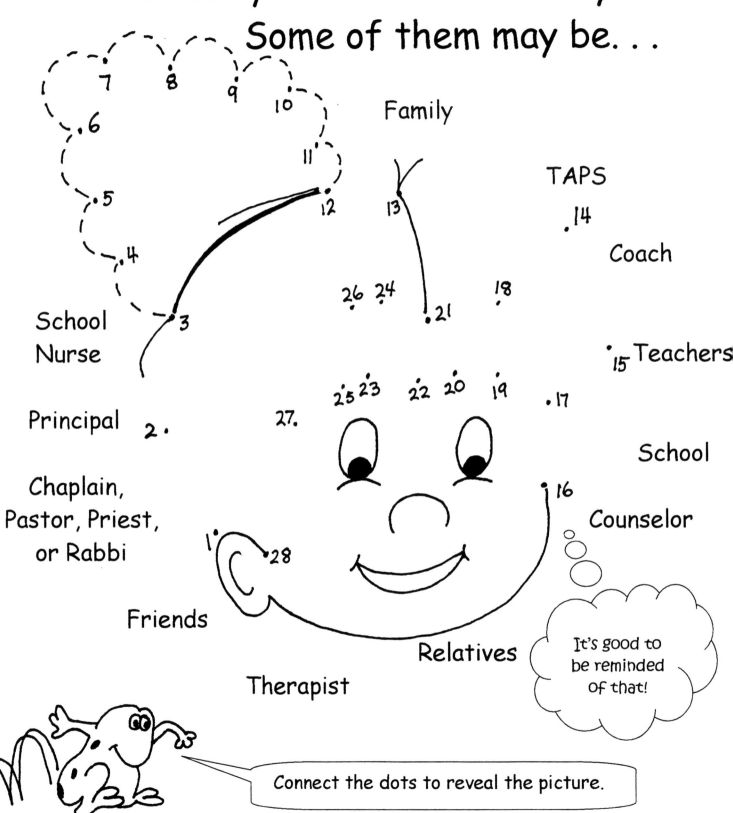

Family

TAPS

Coach

Teachers

School Nurse

Principal

School

Chaplain, Pastor, Priest, or Rabbi

Counselor

Friends

Relatives

It's good to be reminded of that!

Therapist

Connect the dots to reveal the picture.

Along the way, some kids may pick up **the Rocks of Guilt.**
They are heavy and can weigh you down.

It's hard to move forward when you are carrying the feelings of **guilt.**

What Is Guilt?

Guilt is when you feel bad
about something you <u>did</u> or <u>said</u>
and you wish you hadn't. . . .

1 Angry words

2 "I wish you were dead!"

3 "I hate you."

4 I disobeyed you.

5 I let you down.

. . . or you can feel guilt from something you <u>did not</u> say or do, but wish you had.

Not everyone picks up the **Rocks of Guilt** on their grief journey.

If you are carrying some **guilt**,
write in the number of the rock or rocks
(from pages 54 and 55)
that show what you are feeling.

If you have guilt feelings when you think about your special person, write those feelings down here. This is a **great way** to help you lay your Rocks of Guilt down so you can continue to move forward on your journey.

I feel guilty because . . .

_____

_____

_____

_____

_____.

Name some things that you. . .
said to your special person, or
did for your special person that
YOU FEEL GOOD ABOUT.

CARING PERSON AWARD

_____
_____
_____
_____
_____
_____
_____
_____
_____

Share these good things with someone.

ANOTHER LAND OF MOURNING THAT YOU NEED TO TRAVEL THROUGH IS THE

HILLS OF CHANGE

When someone special dies in your life, there are <u>always</u> <u>changes</u>.

Some changes are big, like . . .

☆ Who will make my meals?

☆ Who will drive me to school?

☆ Who will be my best friend?

Circle the face that shows a big change from the others.

And some changes are small, like. . .

☆　I'll get one less card on my Birthday.

☆　I won't be able to watch a movie with my special person.

☆　I can't call him (or her) on the phone.

All the lambs are the same except one. Circle the lamb that has a small change from the others.

They all look the same to me.

Big or small, all of these changes make your life DIFFERENT.

...and sometimes harder.

Draw something that has changed in your life because your special person died.

When someone special dies, your life is different because that person is gone from this life forever.

Grandpa Grandma

Dad Mom Sister Brother Friend

WHO'S MISSING?

Look at each picture. Decide who is missing.

Draw a line from the picture to the person who is missing.

In this land full of "Hills of Change", many things are now going to be different because your special person died. Name 4 things in your life that have changed since his (or her) death.

1. _____

_____

2. _____

_____

3. _____

_____

4. _____

_____

Ask an adult to help you with this page.

Maybe you have thought,

"We are not a family anymore!"

because _____ died.

"Whew, I am glad to know that!"

A FAMILY IS STILL A FAMILY, EVEN IF SOMEONE IN THE FAMILY DIES.

(Draw your happy face)

MAKE YOUR FAMILY AS IT IS NOW.

1. Tear out the next page and fold it on the dotted lines.

2. Cut along the solid lines, but do not cut along the dotted lines.

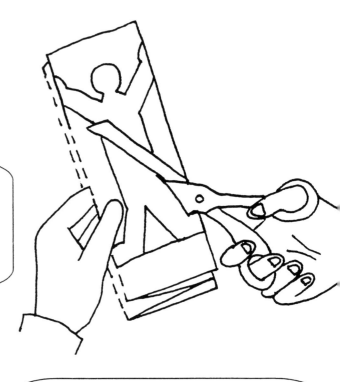

3. Now, unfold your family and color them. If you need to make more, then copy your family on another piece of paper, cut it out and tape them all together.

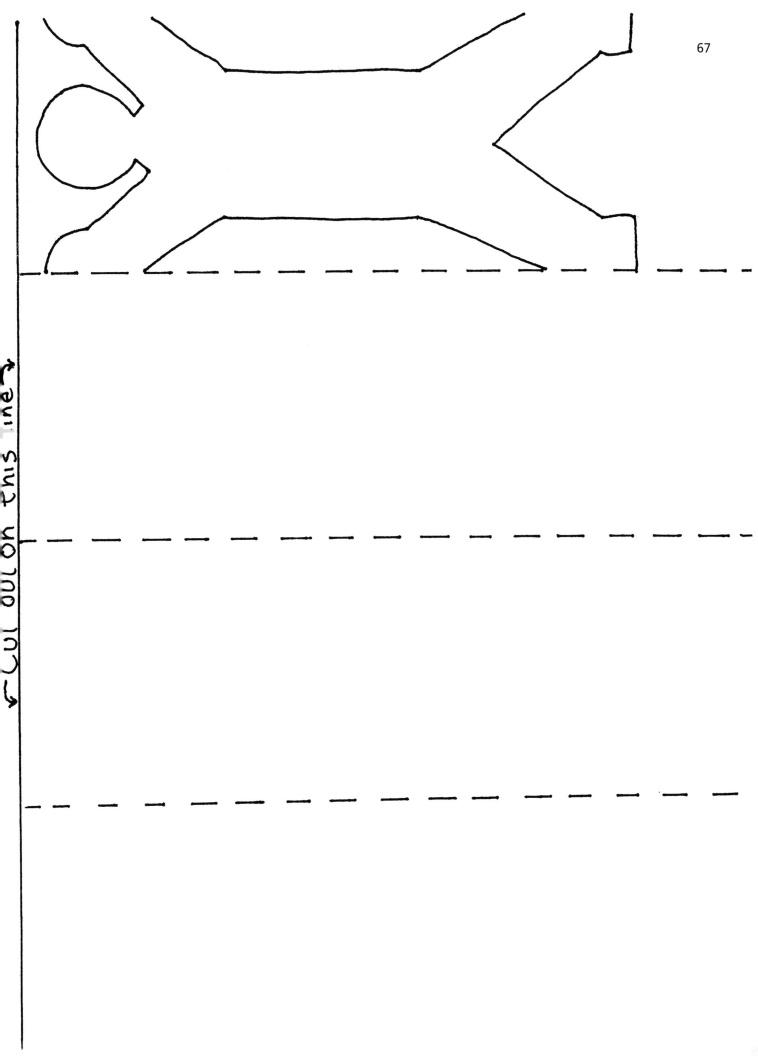

Cut on this line

67

You may have many changes on your grief journey, but life goes on and on almost like normal.

Life goes on day by day, <u>step</u> <u>by</u> <u>step.</u> The same chores and activities are still there to be done.

SPRINGS OF NEW NORMAL this way →

Get up in the morning

I can do this!

Do chores

Go to bed

Do homework

Eat dinner

Get up in the morning

Go to school

Keep doing the things you have to do, even though you don't feel like doing them because you're sad

On the palm leaves below, write the things you do each day that help keep life feeling safe and normal.

Life will never be the same again without your loved one who died, but life can still feel safe and normal again.

The 4th land of mourning that you must travel through is

THE SPRINGS OF NEW NORMAL

Having fun
Enjoying friends
Feeling happy again

NEW NORMAL IS

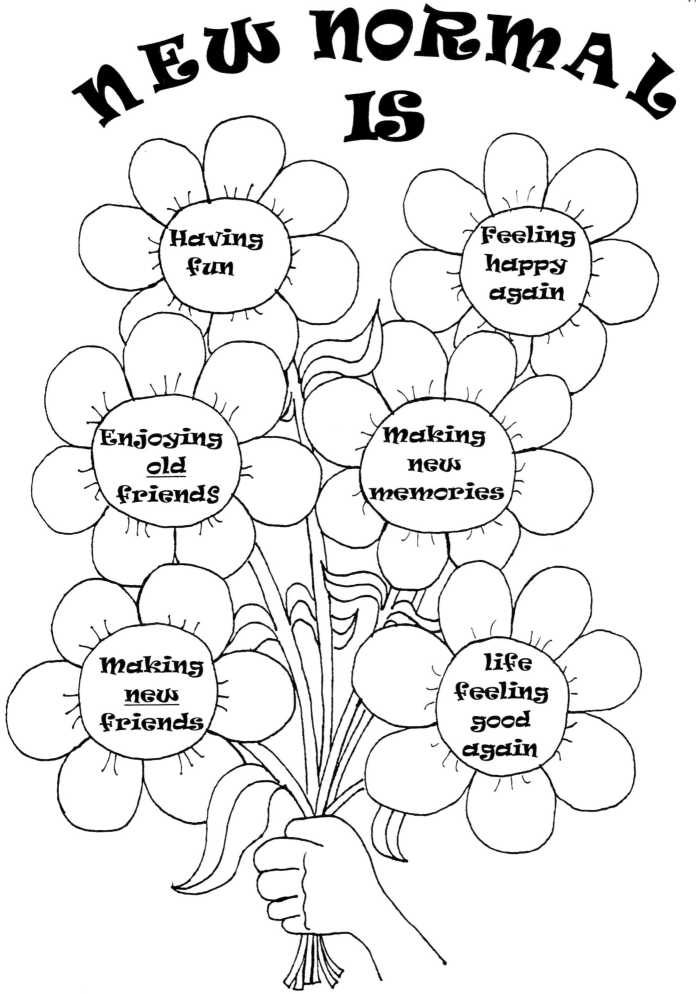

Life won't be the same because your special
person who died isn't with you anymore, BUT. . .
when you talk about
or think about
your special person,
you remember and feel close to that person.

Draw a picture of you and your special
person doing something you did together.

When you reach the "Springs of New Normal", you must say goodbye to your special person. This is important and necessary. A good way to say goodbye is to write a goodbye letter to your special person. ***Write your own letter here:***

	Date _____
●	Dear _____ ,
	I remember when we...
●	
●	You will always be in my heart!
	Goodbye, _____ (your name)

Remember, saying goodbye is <u>not</u> forgetting your loved one.

When your special person died, he/she is no longer with you <u>in person</u>, but is

forever in your heart.

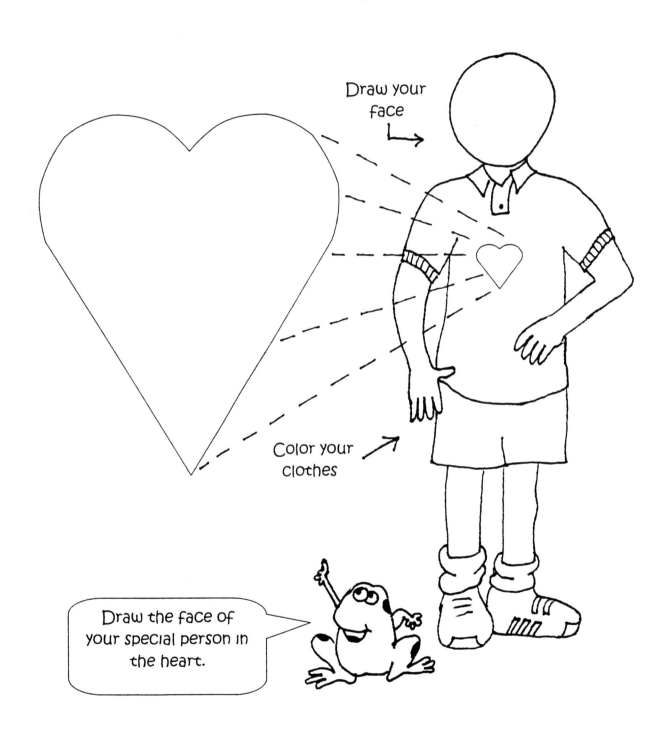

Draw your face

Color your clothes

Draw the face of your special person in the heart.

This is what it means to have your special person in your heart:

"I remember when…

I enjoy remembering the good times with my special person.

When I think of _____, I feel…

I still have feelings for him/her.

"I always liked it when he/she…

I enjoy talking about him/her.

Finish the sentences the way you want to.

There are some important and helpful things you can do to remember that special person who died:

♥ Make a memory book of him/her.

♥ Fly the American flag to honor his/her service to our country.

♥ Place a special picture of him/her in a frame and keep it by your bed.

♥ Light a candle (with the help of an adult) on your special person's birthday.

♥ Draw pictures of him/her.

♥ Look at old photos of him/her.

♥ Talk about memories of him/her with someone.

♥ Give a donation to a charitable organization, like TAPS, in your special person's name.

Know that your special person will always be a part of your life.

Help this person find his way to the LAND OF NEW NORMAL

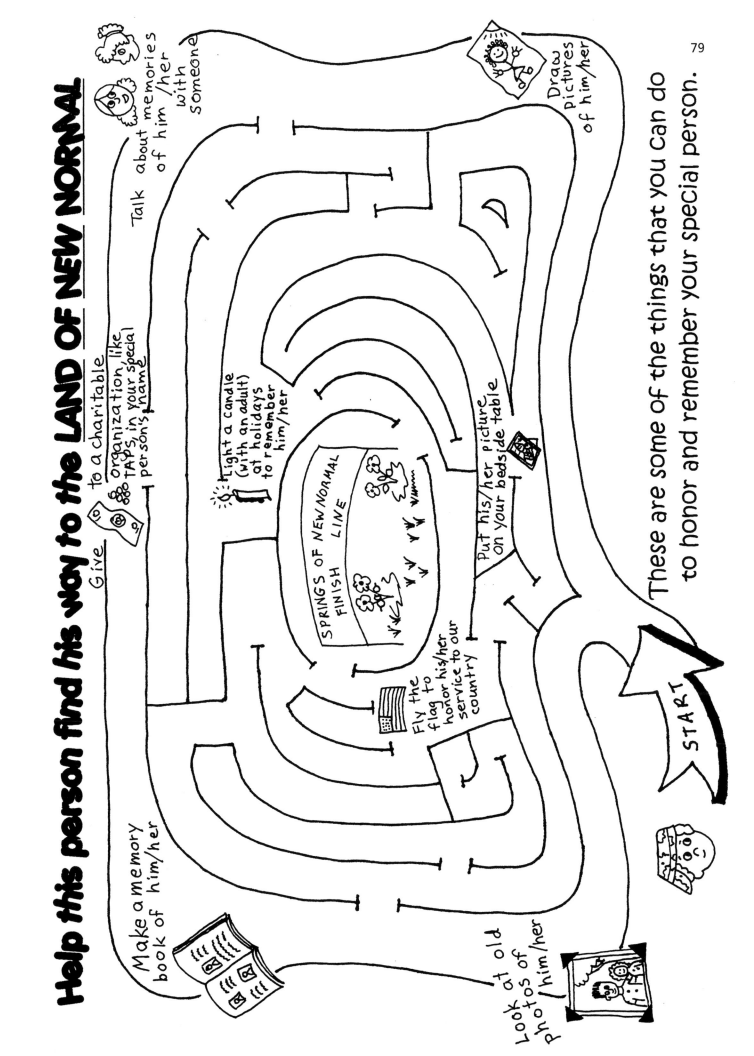

These are some of the things that you can do to honor and remember your special person.

Talk about memories of him/her with someone

Draw pictures of him/her

Give to a charitable organization like TAPS, in your special person's name

Light a candle (with an adult) at holidays to remember him/her

SPRINGS OF NEW NORMAL FINISH LINE

Put his/her picture on your bedside table

Fly the flag to honor his/her service to our country

Make a memory book of him/her

Look at old photos of him/her

START

You made it!

On your grief journey,
it feels so great to feel happy again!

MY MEMORIES

Glue your favorite photos of you and your special person on this page.

WORD SEARCH ANSWERS

INFORMATION, UNDERSTAND, CARED FOR, BLAME, FEAR, DIE, NEVER, SPECIAL

Here are the answers to the word search from page 50:

U	P	O	C	S	I	D	Z	F	U	S	A
A	N	Y	A	O	V	C	Q	E	G	P	K
W	E	D	R	I	R	B	L	A	M	E	M
C	V	A	E	K	M	H	D	R	M	C	W
V	E	P	D	R	D	C	K	R	D	I	E
U	R	F		N	S	W	X	F	R	A	M
M	J	Z	U	E	T	Z	T	Q	L	K	
K	I	N	F	O	R	M	A	T	I	O	N
D	F	T	O	S	K	C	M	N	F	R	T
X	C	N	R	L	X	A	G	E	D	J	K

A KID'S JOURNEY OF GRIEF
official T☆A☆P☆S edition

A handbook for grieving children of military families and the people who surround them.
Written by Susan K. Beeney, R.N. and Jo Anne Chung, B.S.R.N.
Illustrated by Jo Anne Chung

T☆A☆P☆S is America's Veterans Service Organization for the families of those who have died in service to America. All those who are grieving the death of a loved one serving in the armed forces, including children of all ages, are warmly invited and encouraged to participate in our programs of hope and healing. Let us know which services you would like to receive more information about. We're here for you!

☐ Talking to other survivors	☐ Casework Assistance	☐ Peer Mentor Program
☐ Coping with traumatic loss	☐ Casualty Officer Assistance	☐ Weekly Web CHAT
☐ Information about traumatic loss	☐ Chaplain's Assistance	☐ Volunteering
☐ Grief Counseling Assistance	☐ Commander's Briefing	☐ Making a Donation

☐ National Military Survivor Seminar
☐ TEAM **T☆A☆P☆S** in the Marine Corps Marathon
☐ Subscription (free) to **T☆A☆P☆S** magazine
☐ **Good Grief Camp for Young Survivors**

T☆A☆P☆S
Tragedy Assistance Program for Survivors
National Headquarters
1777 F Street, N.W., Suite 600
Washington D.C. 20006
1-800-959-TAPS (8277)
www.TAPS.org
For more information, email us at help@taps.org